AF269447

SOCCER

A&D Xtreme
BOLD HI-LO NONFICTION

An imprint of Abdo Publishing
abdobooks.com

ALEX MONNIG

TAKE IT TO THE XTREME!

GET READY FOR AN EXTREME ADVENTURE! THE PAGES OF THIS BOOK WILL TAKE YOU INTO THE THRILLING WORLD OF SOCCER. WHEN YOU HAVE FINISHED READING THIS BOOK, TAKE THE XTREME CHALLENGE ON PAGE 45 ABOUT WHAT YOU'VE LEARNED!

ABDOBOOKS.COM

Published by Abdo Publishing, a division of ABDO, PO Box 398166, Minneapolis, Minnesota 55439. Copyright © 2023 by Abdo Consulting Group, Inc. International copyrights reserved in all countries. No part of this book may be reproduced in any form without written permission from the publisher. A&D Xtreme™ is a trademark and logo of Abdo Publishing.

Printed in China

102022
012023

Design: Series Designer Kelly Doudna, Mighty Media, Inc.
Production: Mighty Media, Inc.
Editor: Liz Salzmann
Cover Photograph: MICHAEL CAULFIELD/AP Images
Interior Photographs: AP Images, pp. 6–7, 10–11, 42–43; Bernd Weissbrod/AP Images, pp. 26–27; Bob Thomas/Getty Images, pp. 14–15; CARLO FUMAGALLI/AP Images, pp. 16–17; Carmen Jaspersen/AP Images, pp. 40–41; cirtinaclaudiu/Shutterstock Images, pp. 34–35; dpa/AP Images, pp. 12–13; FocusStocker/Shutterstock Images, p. 1; KURT STRUMPF/AP Images, pp. 8–9; MARK J TERRILL/AP Images, pp. 20–21; MARK J. TERRILL/AP Images, pp. 32–33; MICHAEL CAULFIELD/AP Images, pp. 18–19; Mo Khursheed/AP Images, pp. 38–39; moomsabuy/Shutterstock Images, p. 44; ph.FAB/Shutterstock Images, pp. 24–25, 28–29, 30–31; Romain Biard/Shutterstock Images, pp. 4–5; Sarah Reingewirtz/AP Images, pp. 22–23; Wolfgang Kumm/AP Images, pp. 36–37
Design Elements: ayagiz/iStockphoto (hexagon texture); huseyintuncer/iStockphoto (turf); LeArchitecto/iStockphoto (lights); Roman Bykhalets/iStockphoto (dots)

LIBRARY OF CONGRESS CONTROL NUMBER: 2022940527

PUBLISHER'S CATALOGING-IN-PUBLICATION DATA
Names: Monnig, Alex, author.
Title: Soccer / by Alex Monnig
Description: Minneapolis, Minnesota : Abdo Publishing, 2023 | Series: Xtreme moments in sports | Includes online resources and index.
Identifiers: ISBN 9781532199325 (lib. bdg.) | ISBN 9781098274528 (ebook)
Subjects: LCSH: Soccer--Juvenile literature. | Field sports--Juvenile literature. | Soccer--History--Juvenile literature. | Sports--History--Juvenile literature.
Classification: DDC 796.334--dc23

TABLE OF CONTENTS

CHAPTER 1

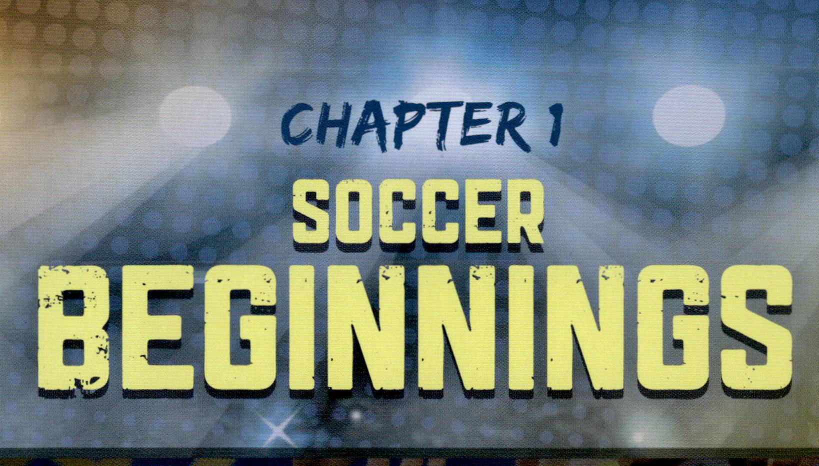

SOCCER BEGINNINGS

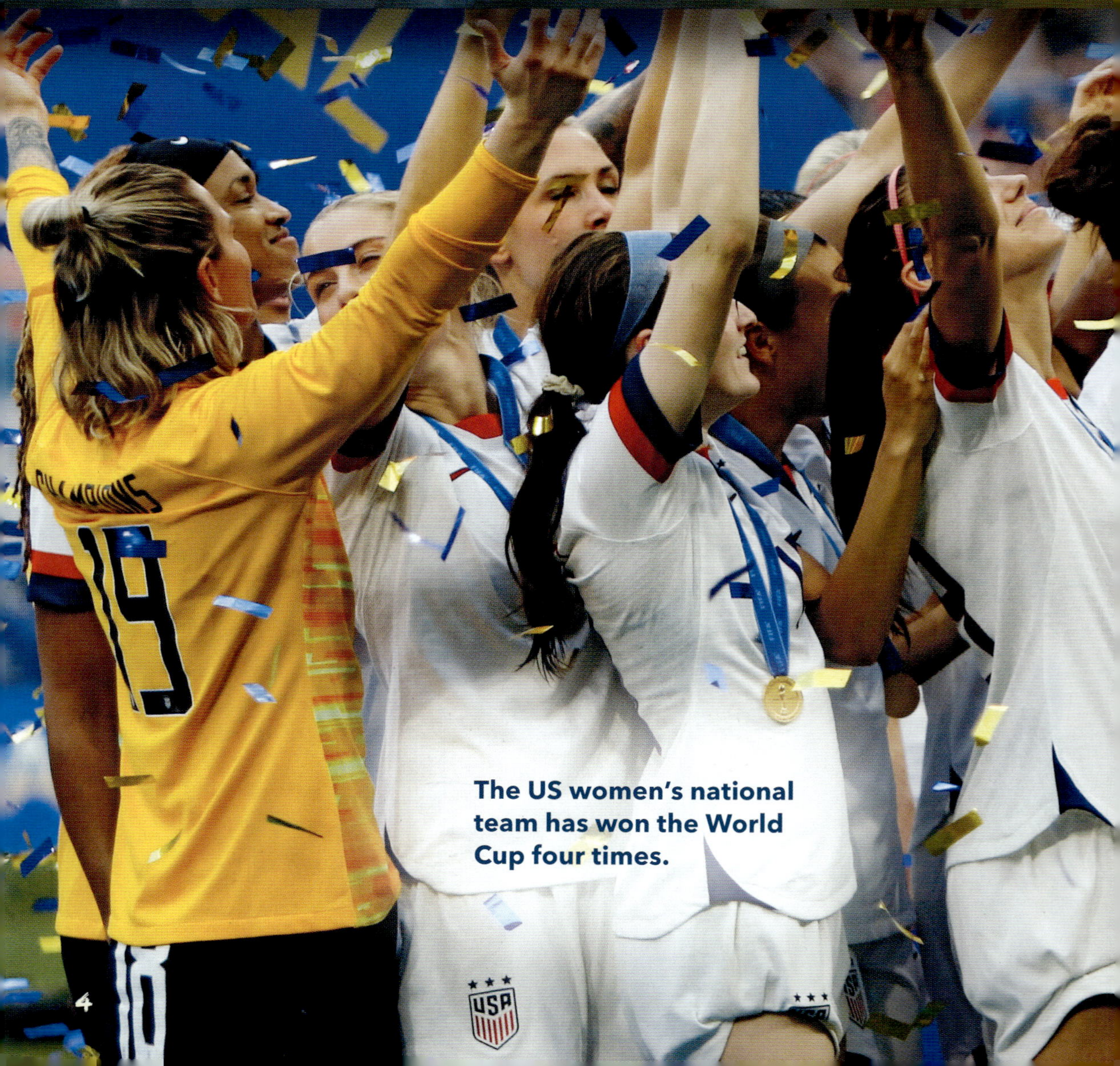

The US women's national team has won the World Cup four times.

Soccer started in 1863 in England. The sport now has many leagues on six continents. In the men's and women's World Cups, national teams play to see which country is the best. These competitions draw millions of soccer-loving fans from around the world.

CHAPTER 2

PELÉ'S
UNFORGETTABLE WORLD CUP

Brazilian **forward** Pelé is often called the best player ever. He played using the *ginga* soccer style. *Ginga* features flashy **dribbling** and passing. And it was on full display at the 1970 World Cup.

XTREME FACT

Pelé was also on the Brazilian teams that won the World Cup in 1958 and 1962. With the victory against Italy in 1970, he became the first player to win three World Cups.

Pelé (*far left*) heads the ball past Italian defender Tarcisio Burgnich to score Brazil's first goal in the World Cup final.

Pelé jumps into teammate Jairzinho's arms after scoring Brazil's first goal in the final game.

Pelé and his amazing teammates dominated the tournament, scoring 19 goals in six matches. Pelé scored four times. His six **assists** set the record for assists during a World Cup.

Pelé's teammates carry him off the field after their World Cup victory over Italy.

Brazil faced Italy in the final match. Brazil won 4–1, with Pelé scoring the first goal and getting **assists** on two others. This was Pelé's final World Cup appearance. He retired from playing seven years later.

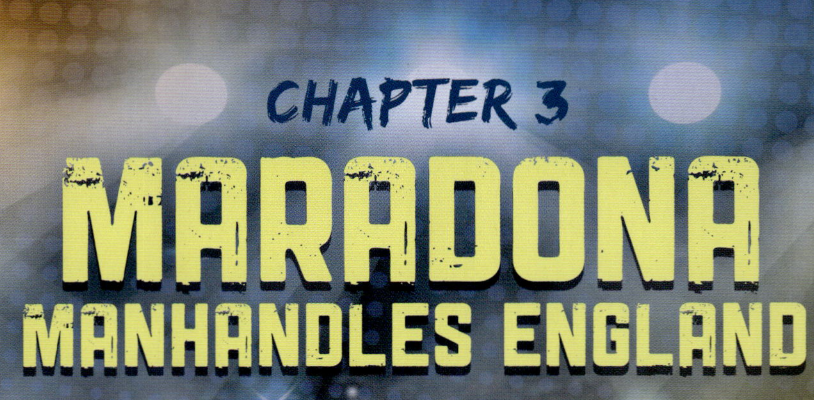

MARADONA MANHANDLES ENGLAND

Diego Maradona was a wizard with the ball at his feet. But the Argentinean **forward** used a different part of his body in the 1986 World Cup quarterfinal match against England. Before the match was over, Maradona would score two of the most iconic goals in soccer history.

Maradona (*second from right*) falls to the ground after being fouled during the match against England.

The goal Maradona scored with his fist
is often called the "Hand of God" goal.

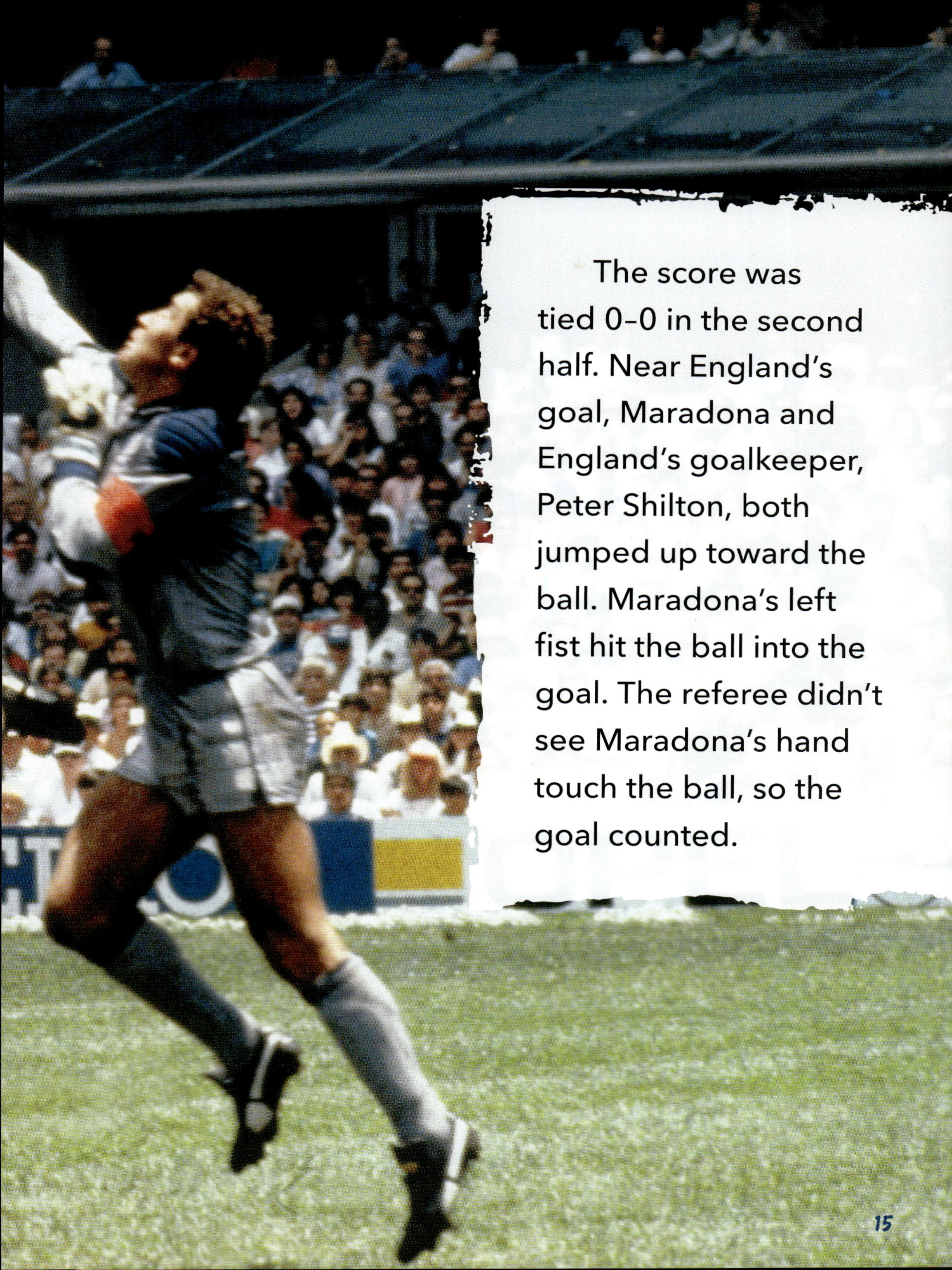

The score was tied 0–0 in the second half. Near England's goal, Maradona and England's goalkeeper, Peter Shilton, both jumped up toward the ball. Maradona's left fist hit the ball into the goal. The referee didn't see Maradona's hand touch the ball, so the goal counted.

Maradona scored another goal four minutes later. It was less **controversial**, but no less amazing. Maradona **dribbled** nearly the entire length of the field, avoiding five English defenders. Then he passed Shilton to score. This is often called the "Goal of the Century."

Maradona celebrates Argentina's World Cup final victory against West Germany.

CHAPTER 4

CHASTAIN LOSES HER SHIRT

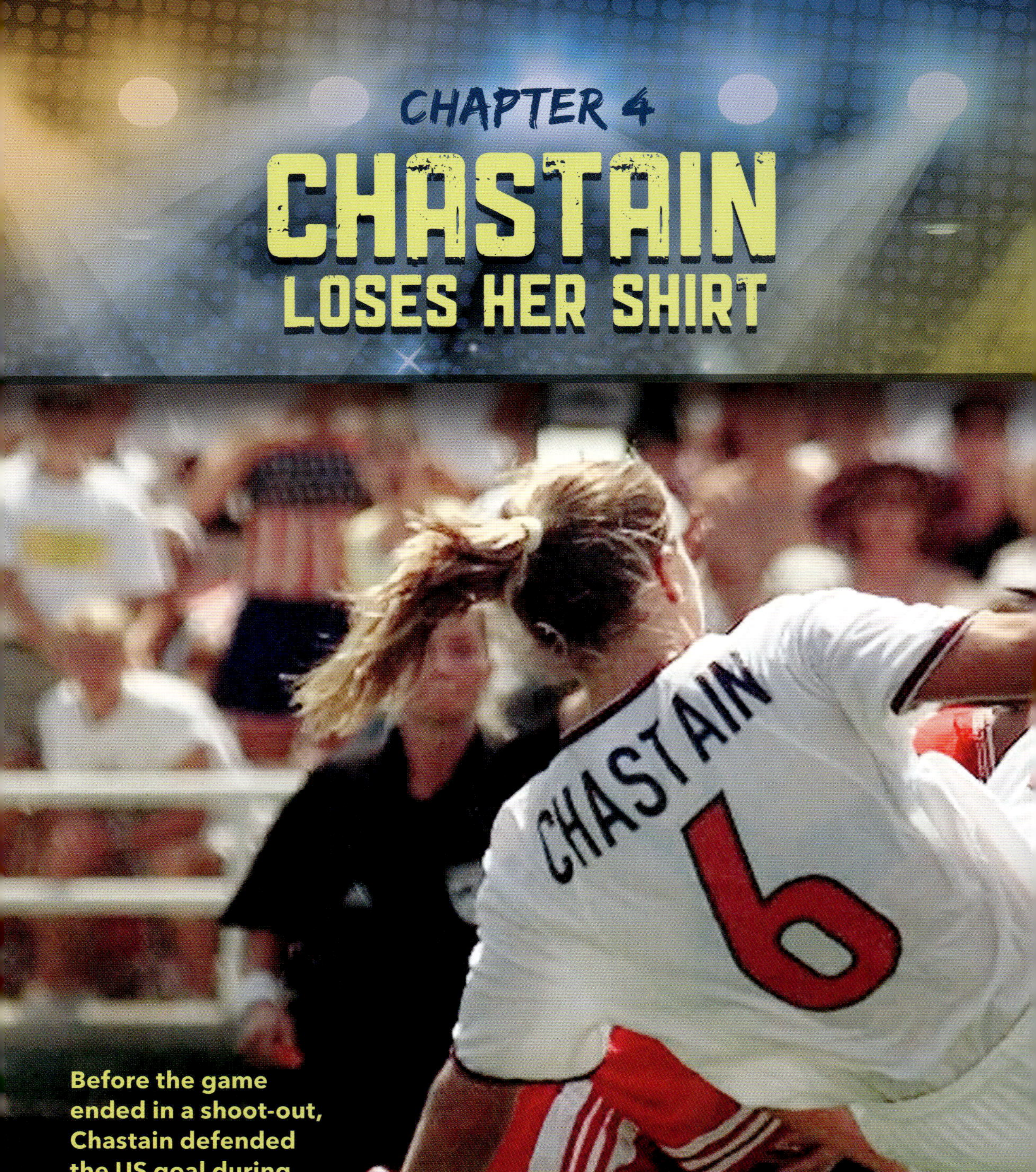

Before the game ended in a shoot-out, Chastain defended the US goal during overtime.

It was the 1999 Women's World Cup final. The game ended in a tie, so it would be decided by **penalty kicks**. Defender Brandi Chastain was the last to kick for the United States. If she scored, Team USA would defeat China and become **champions** for the second time.

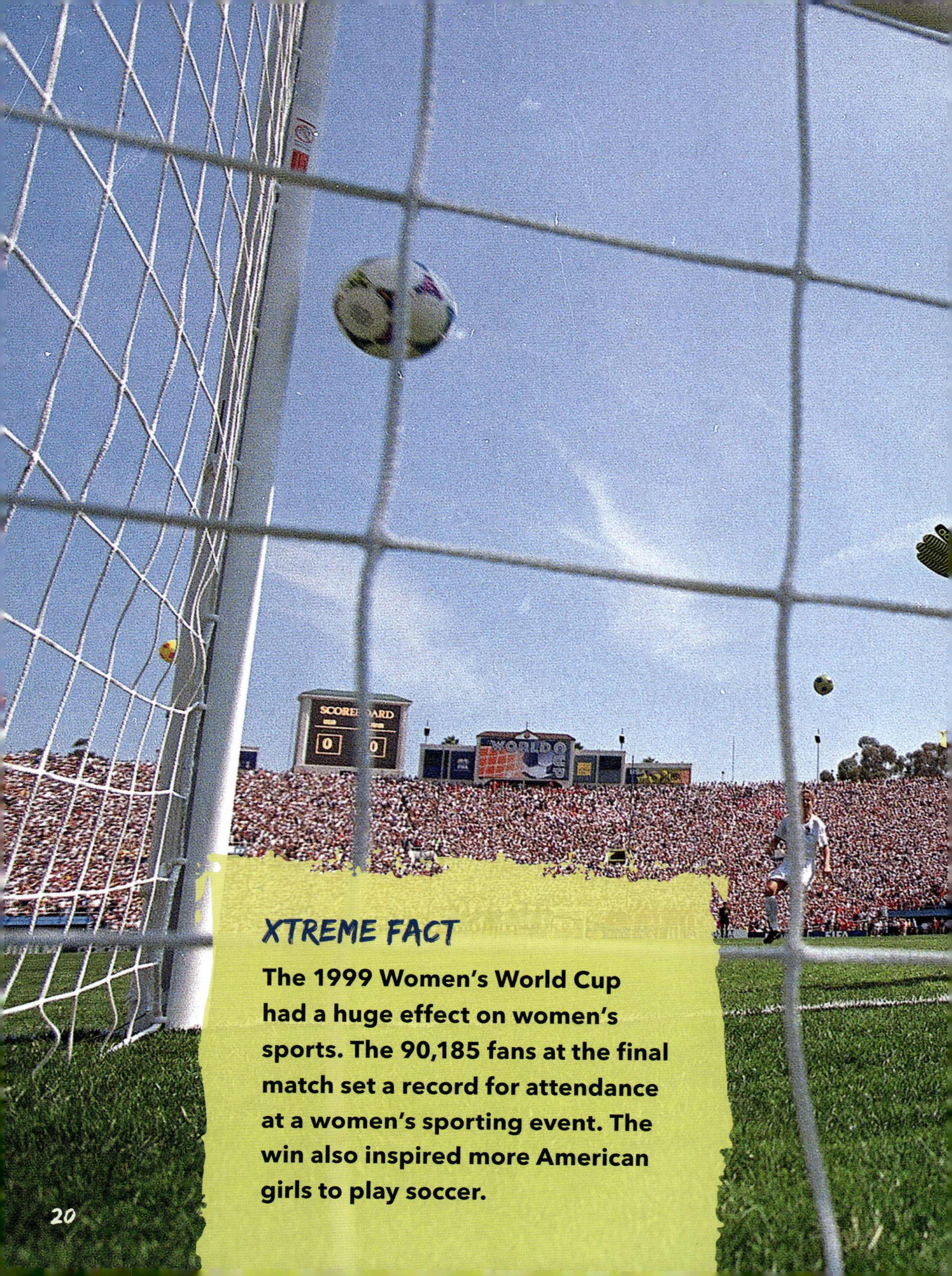

XTREME FACT

The 1999 Women's World Cup had a huge effect on women's sports. The 90,185 fans at the final match set a record for attendance at a women's sporting event. The win also inspired more American girls to play soccer.

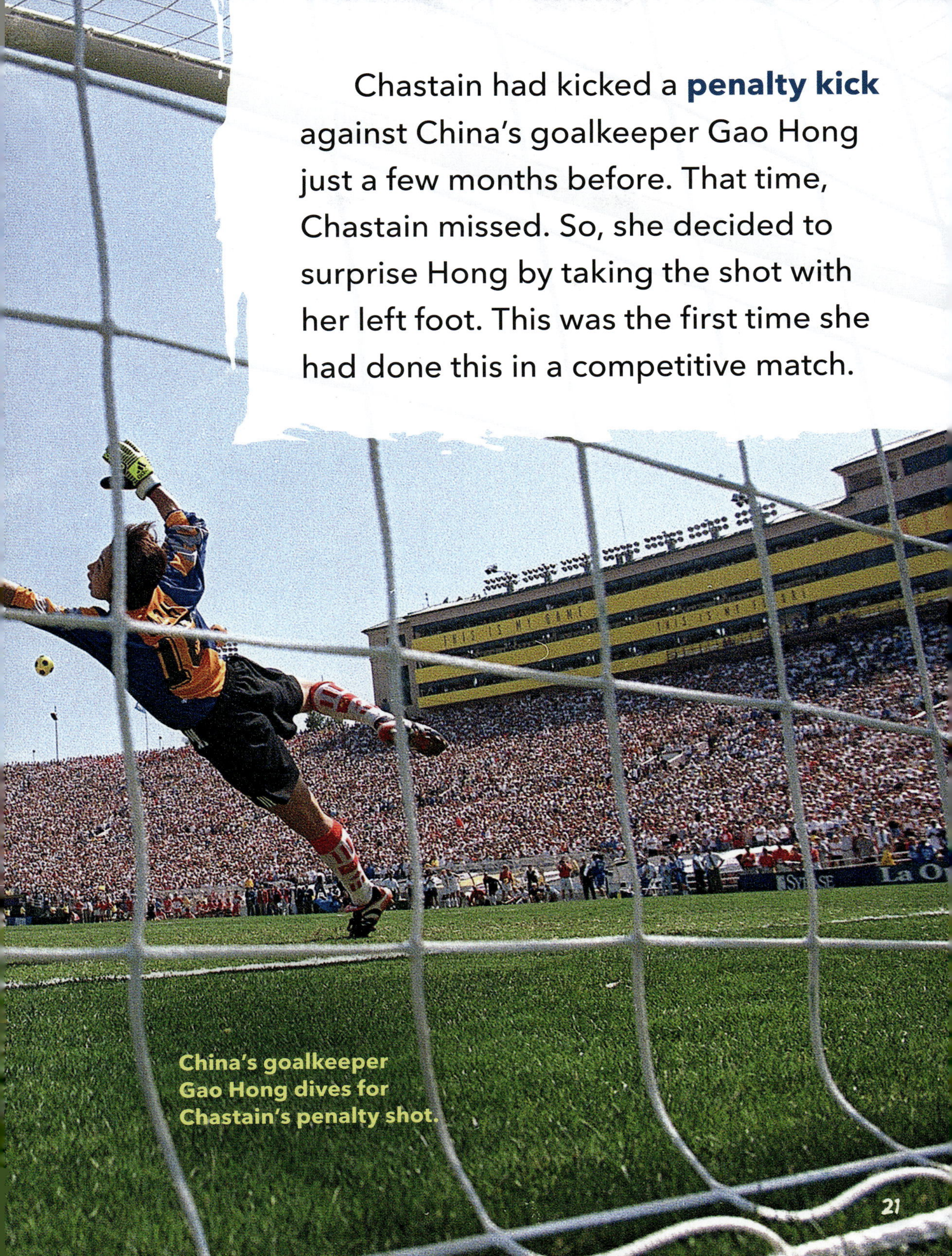

Chastain had kicked a **penalty kick** against China's goalkeeper Gao Hong just a few months before. That time, Chastain missed. So, she decided to surprise Hong by taking the shot with her left foot. This was the first time she had done this in a competitive match.

China's goalkeeper Gao Hong dives for Chastain's penalty shot.

The unexpected move worked! Hong wasn't able to block Chastain's kick. The ball rocketed into the side netting. Chastain dropped to her knees, ripping off her shirt and pumping her fists in the air. It is one of the most memorable moments in World Cup history.

Chastain (*center*) and former teammates pose by a statue of Chastain's iconic World Cup moment.

CHAPTER 5

GREECE STUNS EUROPE

The Greece national team poses before their match against Portugal.

The European **Championships** (Euros) are played every four years. The best national teams from Europe play in it. Many consider the Euros to be second-most important tournament after the World Cup. In 2004, it was held in Portugal. And a very unlikely team won. Many call Greece's triumph the greatest **underdog** victory of all time.

Greece didn't have the exciting skill and flash of the favorite teams. They didn't have popular superstars. But they opened with a surprise win over Portugal. They beat defending **champions** France in the quarterfinals.

Greek forward Angelos Charisteas (*left*) challenges Portugal defender Rui Jorge for the ball.

Then they beat a strong Czech Republic team 1–0 in the semifinals. That set up a rematch with Portugal. The Greeks stunned the host team for a second time with yet another victory to complete the most shocking of title runs. It wasn't flashy. But it worked.

The Greek team celebrates its victory over Portugal in the Euro final.

CHAPTER 6

ZIDANE
LOSES HIS HEAD

French soccer player Zinedine Zidane is one of the most skilled players to ever wear soccer cleats. He was known for his smooth **dribbling** skills, incredible vision, and **pinpoint** passing. But none of this is why people remember Zidane's performance during the 2006 World Cup.

Zidane follows through on a kick during a 2004 match against England.

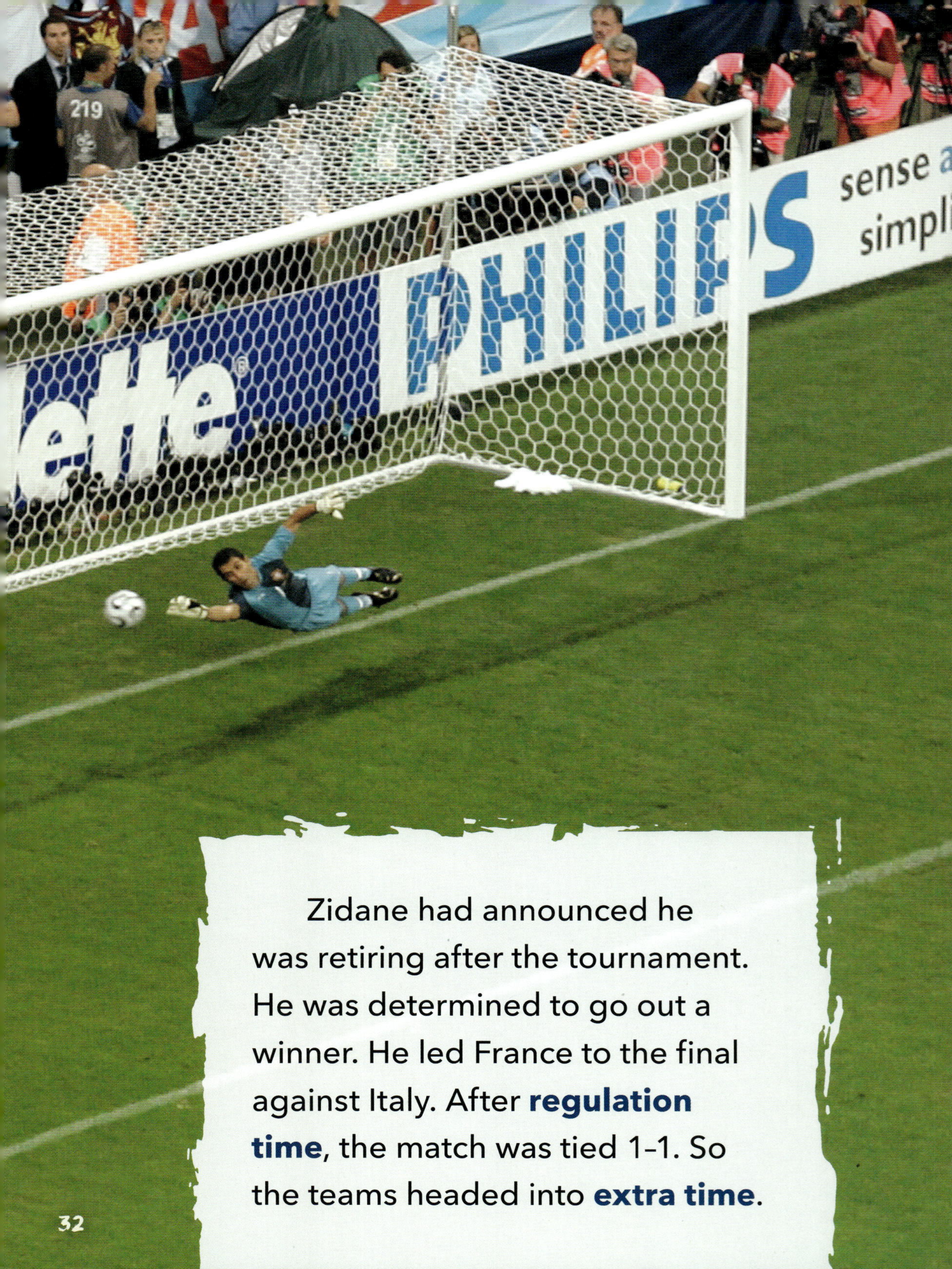

Zidane had announced he was retiring after the tournament. He was determined to go out a winner. He led France to the final against Italy. After **regulation time**, the match was tied 1–1. So the teams headed into **extra time**.

Zidane scored a penalty goal in the semifinal game against Portugal.

With 10 minutes left before potential **penalty kicks**, Zidane made a poor decision. As Zidane passed Italian defender Marco Materazzi, Materazzi insulted Zidane's sister. Zidane turned and headbutted Materazzi in the chest. The Italian fell to the ground.

A sculpture of Zidane's
famous headbutt was
unveiled in France in 2012.

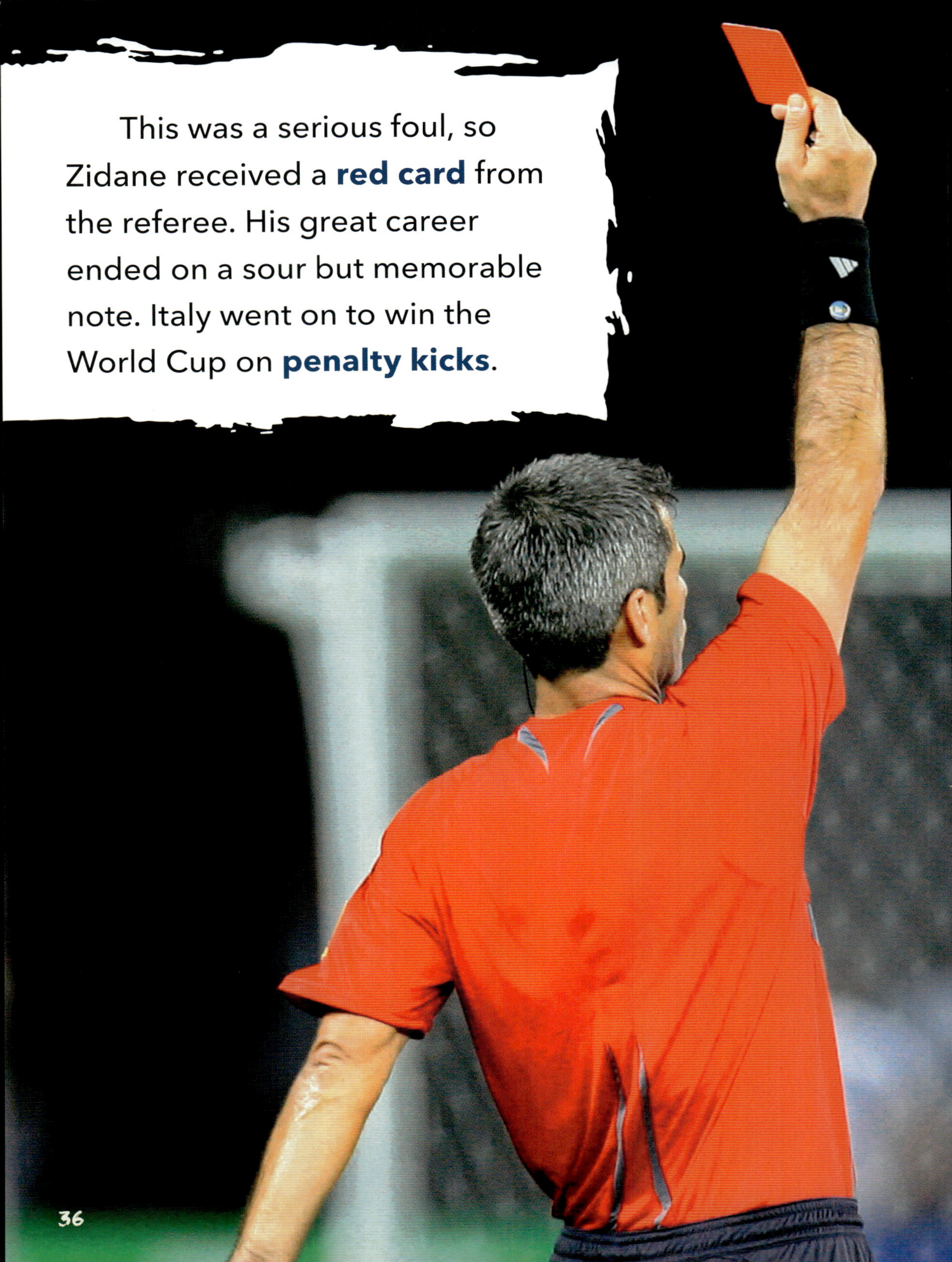

This was a serious foul, so Zidane received a **red card** from the referee. His great career ended on a sour but memorable note. Italy went on to win the World Cup on **penalty kicks**.

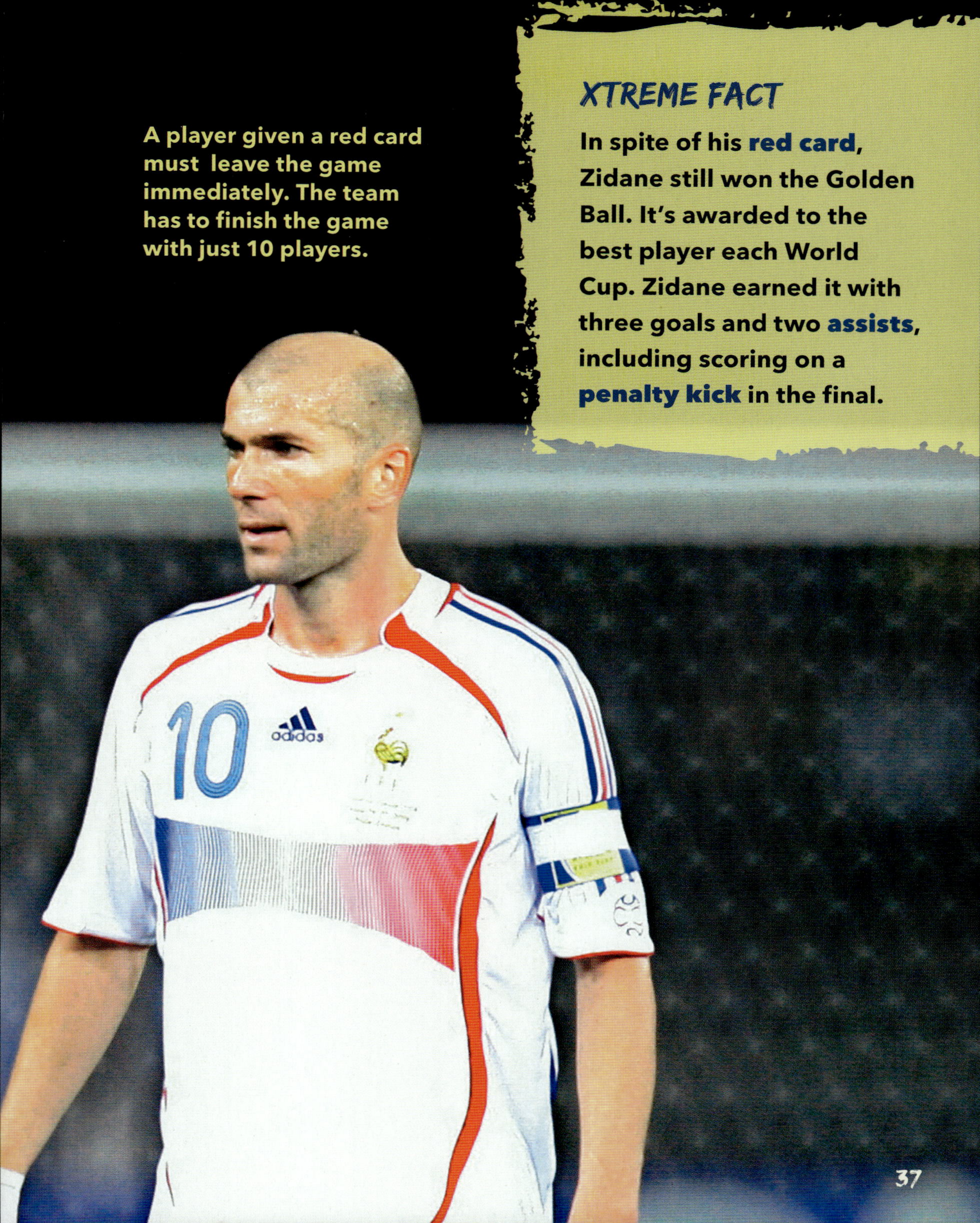

A player given a red card must leave the game immediately. The team has to finish the game with just 10 players.

CHAPTER 7

HAT TRICK HERO

In 2015, the US women were looking to even the score with Japan. Team USA had lost the 2011 World Cup final to Japan on **penalty kicks**. Now the two teams were meeting for the trophy again. And US **forward** Carli Lloyd made sure the rematch turned out differently.

Lloyd (#10) battles Japan's Saki Kumagai for the ball during the second half of the final.

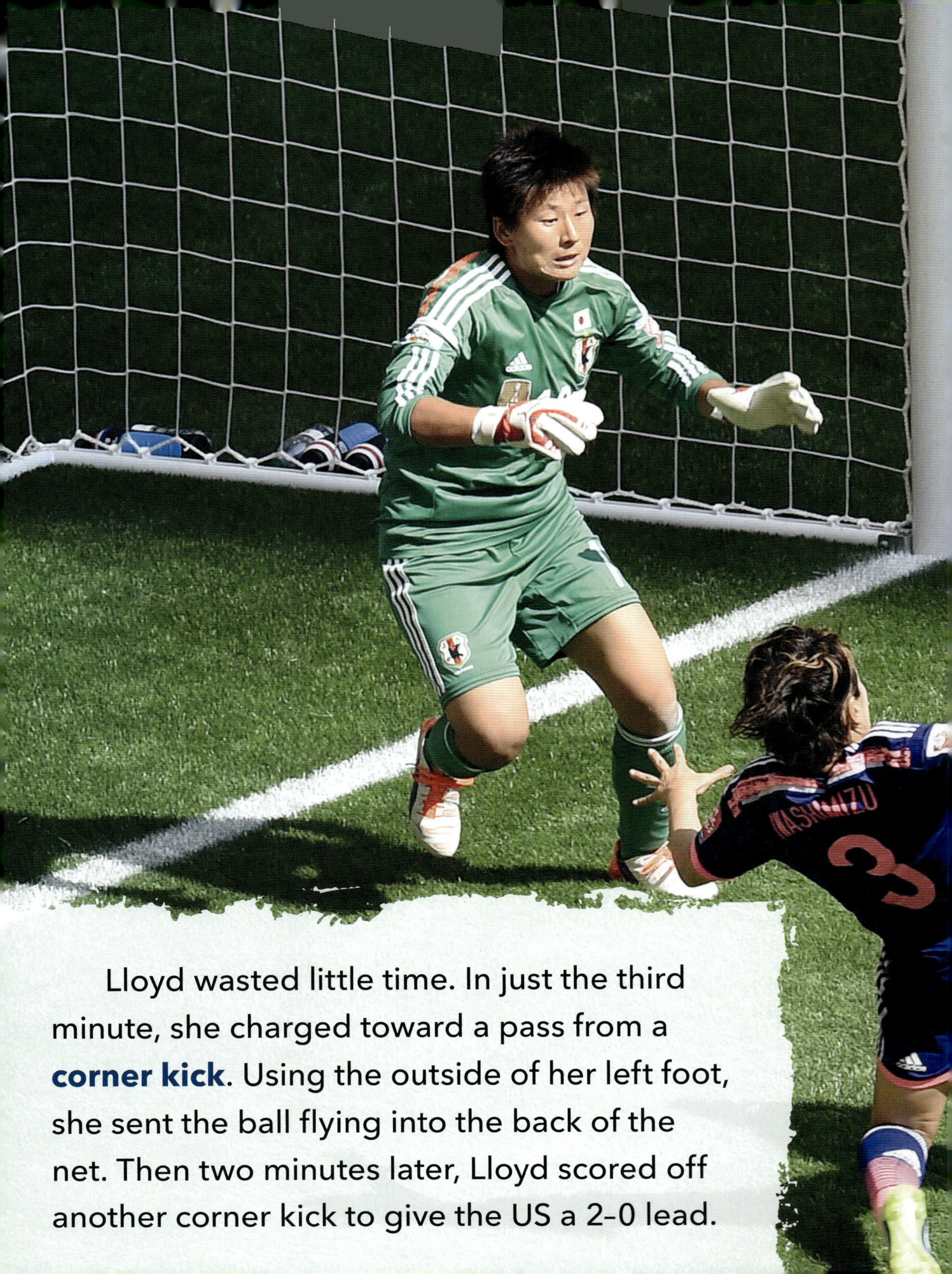

Lloyd wasted little time. In just the third minute, she charged toward a pass from a **corner kick**. Using the outside of her left foot, she sent the ball flying into the back of the net. Then two minutes later, Lloyd scored off another corner kick to give the US a 2–0 lead.

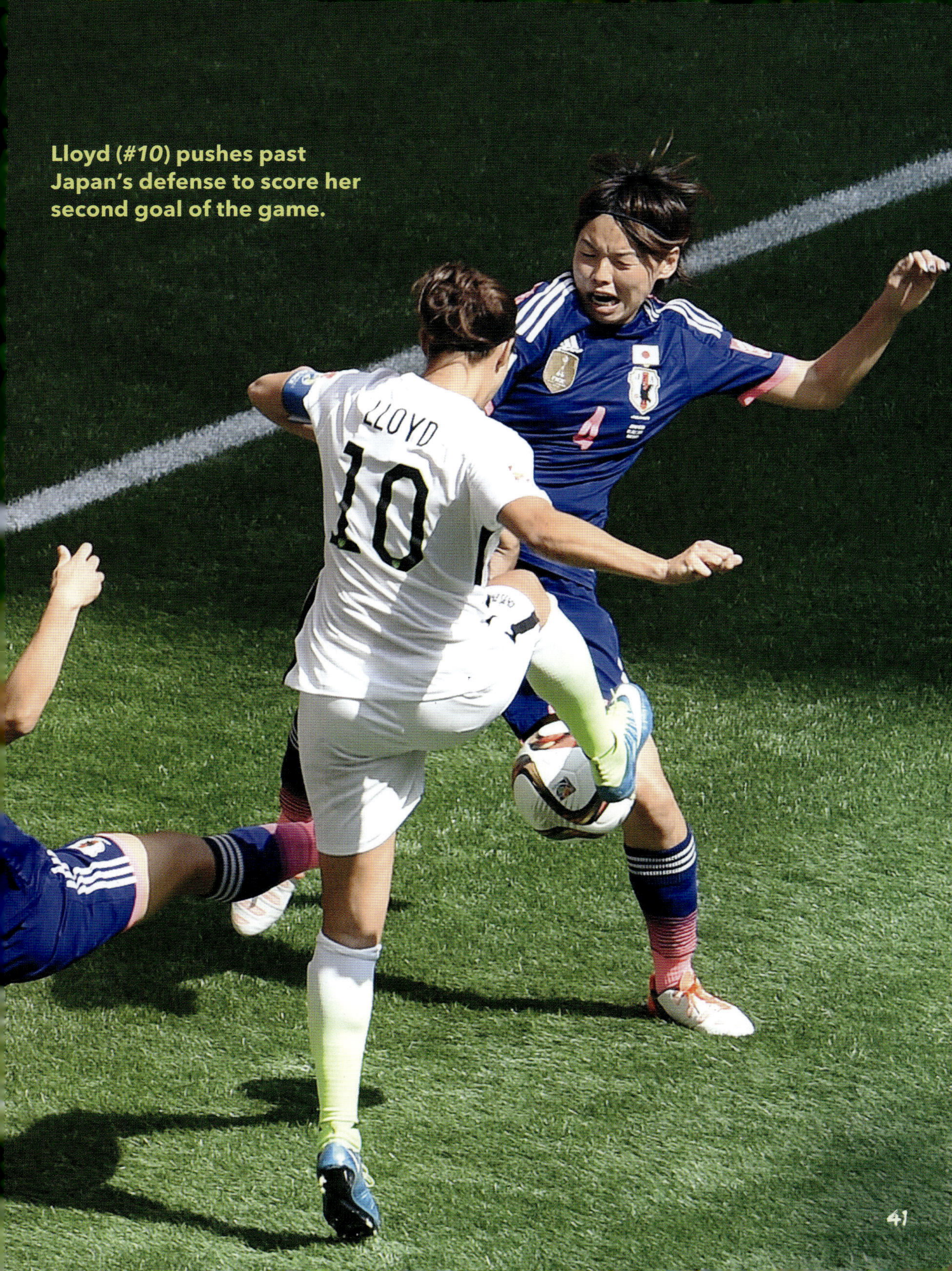

Lloyd (*#10*) pushes past Japan's defense to score her second goal of the game.

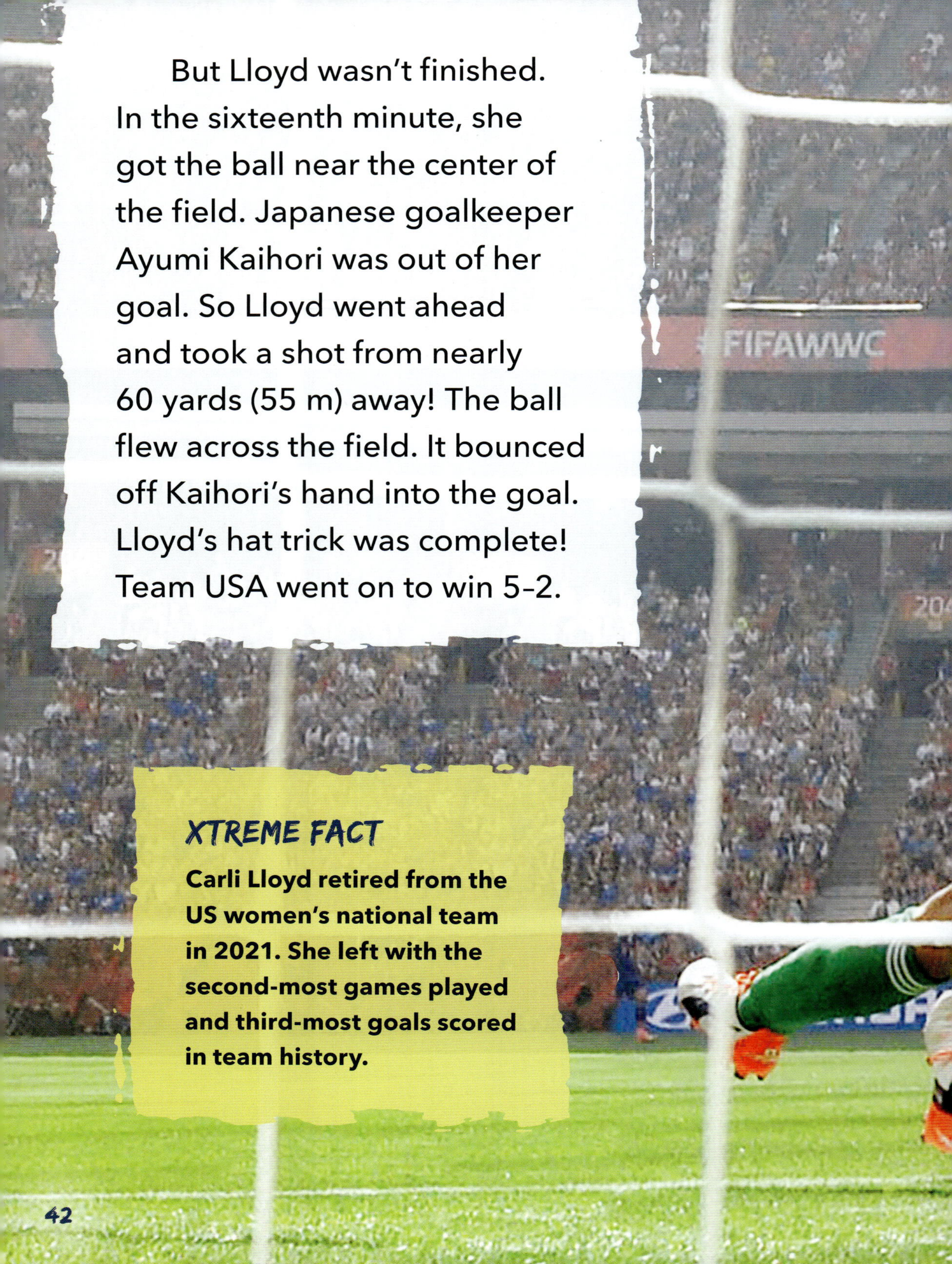

But Lloyd wasn't finished. In the sixteenth minute, she got the ball near the center of the field. Japanese goalkeeper Ayumi Kaihori was out of her goal. So Lloyd went ahead and took a shot from nearly 60 yards (55 m) away! The ball flew across the field. It bounced off Kaihori's hand into the goal. Lloyd's hat trick was complete! Team USA went on to win 5–2.

XTREME FACT

Carli Lloyd retired from the US women's national team in 2021. She left with the second-most games played and third-most goals scored in team history.

Lloyd's third goal slips past the fingers of Japan's goalkeeper, Ayumi Kaihori.

CHAPTER 8

THE FUTURE
OF SOCCER

Many sports are only played in a handful of countries. But soccer is a truly global sport played in hundreds of countries. Stars such as Mohamed Salah, Kylian Mbappé, and Samantha Kerr continue to reinvent the sport with their amazing skills. The future looks bright for soccer fans around the world.

XTREME CHALLENGE

TAKE THE QUIZ BELOW AND
PUT WHAT YOU'VE LEARNED TO THE TEST!

1) Why was the 1999 Women's World Cup final match so important?

2) Who did Carli Lloyd score a hat trick against in the 2015 Women's World Cup final?

3) Would you rather have been part of the Greece team that won the 2005 European Championships or the Brazilian team that won the 1970 World Cup?

4) How did Diego Maradona score the "Hand of God" goal?

5) Whose arms did Pelé jump into after scoring the first goal of the 1970 World Cup final?

GLOSSARY

assist—in sports, an action of a player that allows a teammate to score a goal.

championship—a game, a match, or a race held to find a first-place winner. The winner of a championship is called a champion.

controversial—involving an argument or debate over a decision or outcome.

corner kick—a free kick that is taken from a corner of a soccer field. It is awarded to an attacker when a defender plays the ball out-of-bounds over the end line.

dribble—to run down a soccer field while moving the ball with short kicks.

extra time—in soccer, two additional 15-minute periods of play that occur if the score is tied when the game clock runs out.

forward—a player positioned near the opponent's goal whose main job is to score.

penalty kick—in soccer, a free kick that is taken from 12 yards (11 m) in front of the goal. It is allowed for certain types of fouls. Penalty kicks are also used to determine the winner of a match if the score is tied.

pinpoint—located or aimed with great precision or accuracy.

red card—in soccer, a penalty given to a player who makes certain types of fouls. The player has to leave the game and cannot be replaced.

regulation time—the normal time allowed for a game such as soccer or basketball.

underdog—a person or team thought to have little chance of winning.

ONLINE RESOURCES

To learn more about soccer, please visit **abdobooklinks.com** or scan this QR code. These links are routinely monitored and updated to provide the most current information available.

INDEX